Seven Spirals

A Chakra Sutra for Kids

Deena Haiber

Aimee MacDonald

Mushroom Hollow Press

For information, please contact:
Mushroom Hollow Press
28517 Meadowrush Way,
Wesley Chapel, FL 33543
813/361-1002.

The text of this book is set in Magician, Worcester and Papyrus

Publisher's Cataloging in Publication Data
Haiber, Deena.
Seven spirals : a chakra sutra for kids / Deena Haiber and Aimee MacDonald.
p. cm.
Summary: Through real-life situations, seven kids learn about the chakras and their meanings.

ISBN 13: 978-0-615-24185-2
ISBN 10: 0-615-24185-9

1. Chakras—Juvenile fiction. 2. Spirituality—Juvenile fiction.
    I.   Haiber, Deena. II. MacDonald, Aimee. III. Title.

PZ5 .H35 Se 2009

813.6

2008936050

Thanks...

Seven Spirals began on a lark–a project we undertook just for fun, and for the purposes of getting ourselves, two stay-at-home, homeschooling moms, through the dog days of a Florida summer. It has since grown a bit, and we have many folks to thank for that:

First, the husbands and kids. Many thanks for allowing us to slack on our mom and wife duties and for eating a lot of takeout, not complaining too loudly when we hogged the computers and dining room tables, and for just generally being great. So, from Deena, thanks to Christian, Gillian and Claire. And from Aimee, thanks to Jay, Gresham, Bronwyn and Quinlan. We love you guys.

To the Silver Spiral gang -- thanks so much for your love and encouragement, it has meant more to us than you know. Andrea, we used your soaps before each and every attempt at art – and, you know, I think they worked!

For two newbie writer/illustrators, with very limited time and even more limited funds-- having talented friends is indispensable – and we certainly lucked out in that department. Thanks very much to Sheila Dougherty, Nate Etheridge and Jennie Spalti for helping us so much in their areas of expertise–we certainly couldn't have done it without you. We'd also like to thank Ms. Rachel Longstaff, Saint Leo's cataloging-librarian-extraordinaire for being so generous with her time and assistance.

Finally, thanks to Mike for being Aimee's sounding board, and to Allan MacDonald for his generous gifts of pencils, and an ancestry of artistic talent.

Author's note: On each Chakra page, we've included both the Chakra's name in English (upper right) and in Sanskrit (lower left).

Root

Muladhara

owan woke up *too* early one morning, a little cranky, and just this side of grumpy.

"Finally, I'm finished with all those chores!" she thought, picking a nice shady spot under her favorite tree.

Rowan did love being outside. What she didn't know was that Tree loved her being there, too. So much so, in fact, that when Rowan sat very still and made her mind very quiet, she could hear Tree do something that was very rare: she *spoke*.

"Mornin', Darlin'," Tree said. "The sun is rising, it is such a sweet and lovely day, my roots are just dancing!"

Rowan was startled, but only for a second.
She laughed and thought a little.
"I wish I had roots, Tree. Then I wouldn't have to run around and do chores all the time!"
"Well, you most certainly do have roots, Rowan."
Rowan looked up, not at all sure *what* Tree was talking about.
"What do you mean?" Rowan asked.
Tree mulled it over for a moment.
"Let me think how I can tell it to you, child, so you'll understand... did you have a good breakfast this morning?"
"Sure did."
"Did you sleep in a nice comfy bed last night?"
"Yeah," Rowan remembered, "I *love* my bed."
"Well, sounds to me like you've got everything you need! So what worries you got, little one?"
Rowan smiled.
And she knew that Tree was right.

Rowan breathed in as Tree breathed out. The ground felt a little cool to sit on, but Rowan didn't care. Soon she couldn't even tell where she ended and that ground began. The wind tousled her hair and rustled Tree's leaves...

...and they stayed there like that for a long time.

Sacral

Svadhisthana

hat same morning, as the sun was peeking up, someone else was peeking, too. That'd be Rowan's little brother, Sam. He had started his day with a scrumptious breakfast of crispy toast dripping with golden honey.

Mmmmm... he licked his lips just remembering that delicious stuff. But, no time for more—he had important matters to attend to.

Sam ran as fast as he could toward the barn, gulping fresh, clean lungfuls of air—he loved going fast! Soon, he found what he was looking for—there it was, the bluejay's nest he had been watching for weeks. He peered into the nest—would there be any change? You'd better believe there was. The eggs had hatched!

Sam gazed with wonder at the tiny chicks, hungrily waiting for their mama to bring their wormy breakfast. Smiling at that gross thought, Sam heard something—a faint buzzing—was there a beehive somewhere up in the rafters? Then he noticed a mama cat happily curled up in the sun as her babies had their breakfast. It seemed mamas and their babies were everywhere, and the whole barn was buzzing with life that morning!

Sam wished he could stay longer, but soon he had to say goodbye and head back home. He and Rowan had a lot to do that day. First up was a show at the community center starring one of their best friends, Nadja.

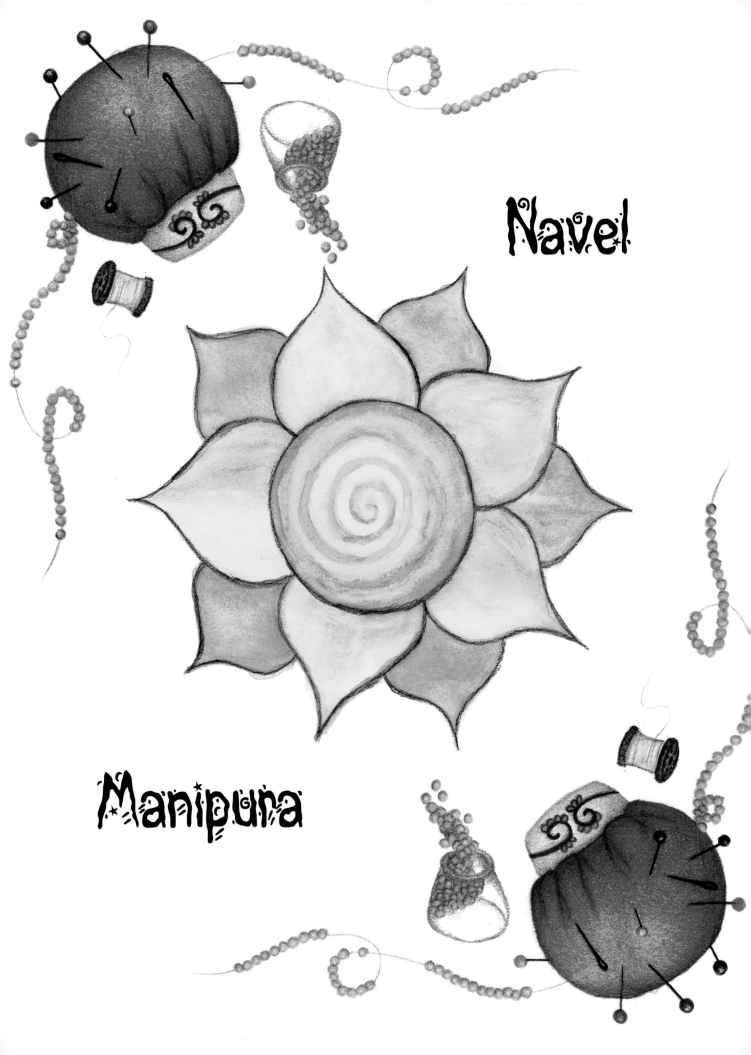

Navel

Manipura

usic filled the air as Nadja took the stage. She whirled and twirled to the sound of the drum and sitar. Dancing now, she was lovely and so sure of herself. But last night had been a different story.

"I can't do it, I can't dance in front of all those people!" Nadja fretted. She had never been this nervous.

Grandmama smiled. "Come here, Nadja, let's talk for a moment. Do you know how many amber beads are on your costume, little one? I don't even know myself, but I swear, there must be… Well, a lot! And do you know what I thought about as I sewed each one? I thought, 'How beautiful my Nadja will be. How happy she will make people with her wonderful dancing, and how good *she* will feel about that!'"

Nadja laughed and she did feel a little better.

Then her older sister paid her the best compliment of all.

"Nadja, if you like, I will paint a mendhi design around your belly button for good luck! You must hold very still. And breathe in and out as slowly as you can."

Nadja did just that—she didn't want to disturb her sister's steady hand. With each slow, patient breath, she felt a little more calm.

Finally, when Nadja's mama and papa kissed her and told her how proud they were, she knew she would be able to dance...

...and dance she did.

Heart

Anahata

alking home from the performance, Henry and his friends noticed something that stopped them in their tracks.

Their neighbor, Mr. Randal, was raking leaves, and having a very hard time of it. Henry remembered that the older man's back sometimes hurt.

"Hey, Mr. Randal—can I give you a hand?"

"Henry! Just the guy I wanted to see. Sure, I'd love a hand—or two if you got 'em!" Henry laughed—he and Mr. Randal always got each other's jokes.

Henry's friends agreed to help, too. Together, they finished those leaves in no time flat.

Later, Mrs. Randal served them all tea and her special lemon cookies.

"Thank you so much!" she said to them all.
"Henry, you're a good friend to us. Don't know what we'd do without you!"

Henry smiled. He thought the Randals were great friends, too, and he liked listening to their stories of days gone by. It made him feel good to help his friends. And the cookies weren't bad, either.

"I still remember the day we met," Mrs. Randal began. "I would skate at the roller rink every Saturday..."

"...and so did I," continued Mr. Randal, "and I noticed she always wore cute little red pom poms on her skates. I asked her to skate with me, but she wouldn't!"

"Oh, go on!" Mrs. Randal laughed.
"It's true, you wouldn't!" Mr. Randal laughed.
"But I kept at it. When she finally did agree to skate with me, I almost fell and dragged her down with me. She didn't mind, though. She was in love with me already, you see..."

throat

Vishudda

hat evening, the camping trip they'd all been looking forward to was finally happening. A few of the kids had been camping before, but this was the first time for most. As Thomas and his dad hiked up the trail back to their campsite, they heard a gray owl singing softly to a brown one, high in the trees.

"Can they really talk to each other, Dad?" Thomas asked, pointing up to the owls.
"Sure," said Dad. "All creatures talk in *some* way."

"What do they eat? How do they sleep up there
 without falling out of the tree? And what about those berries we saw back there, do owls eat those? Can *we* eat 'em?"

Dad smiled at Thomas.

"Do I ask too many questions, Dad?"

"Nope," Dad laughed, "you ask just the right number of questions."

"Well, let's see here," Dad said, "I think owls eat mice and bugs, and other little animals. Probably not berries, though, I think they're carnivores. And I'm pretty sure they do sleep in trees."

"They must have awesome balance to be able to do that!" Thomas said. "Yes, they must," Dad said. "Let's look that up when we get home."

Forehead

Ajna

he next day, the kids discovered something—there was a lake next to their campsite! And that's just what Fiona was running toward, as she bounded her way down the hill to meet her friends. Or *were* they? For a moment, they looked somehow *different*.

Was that Nadja, or a sneaky wood troll? Henry, or the world's most death-defying trapeze artist? Soon two Samurai (also known as Rowan and Sam) began to circle each other in a battle for honor, justice—and the last cookie in the cooler.

Down at the lake's edge, *something* was happening. "It rises!" shouted Fiona, as the wind kicked up, and the surface of the lake was disturbed by ripple after ripple. "There's a loch monster in there, all right! It's been sleeping for four million years... and it just...woke...up."

Her friends looked at each other with gleaming eyes, and made sure they were battle-ready.

"There's no way to tell if it's friend or foe just yet," yelled Fi. "Best be on our guards!"

Brandishing her sword, Fi ran toward the lake...

After all, she had always wanted
to be a knight...

Crown

Sahasrara

ater that night (much later than they were *usually* allowed to stay up, anyway), Casey and the other campers were tired and happy. Before they settled down to yet another round of s'mores and ghost stories, they decided to go for a walk to find out which sparkled more, the moonlit lake or the starry sky.

Casey closed her eyes and just listened. She loved being out here with her friends, by the water and under the stars. Out here, stuff like math tests, clothes, arguments with her sister—just didn't seem to matter very much. When she looked up at that great big sky, Casey knew that she was only a tiny grain of sand on a *very* big beach—and, yet, at the same time, she was all that ever was.

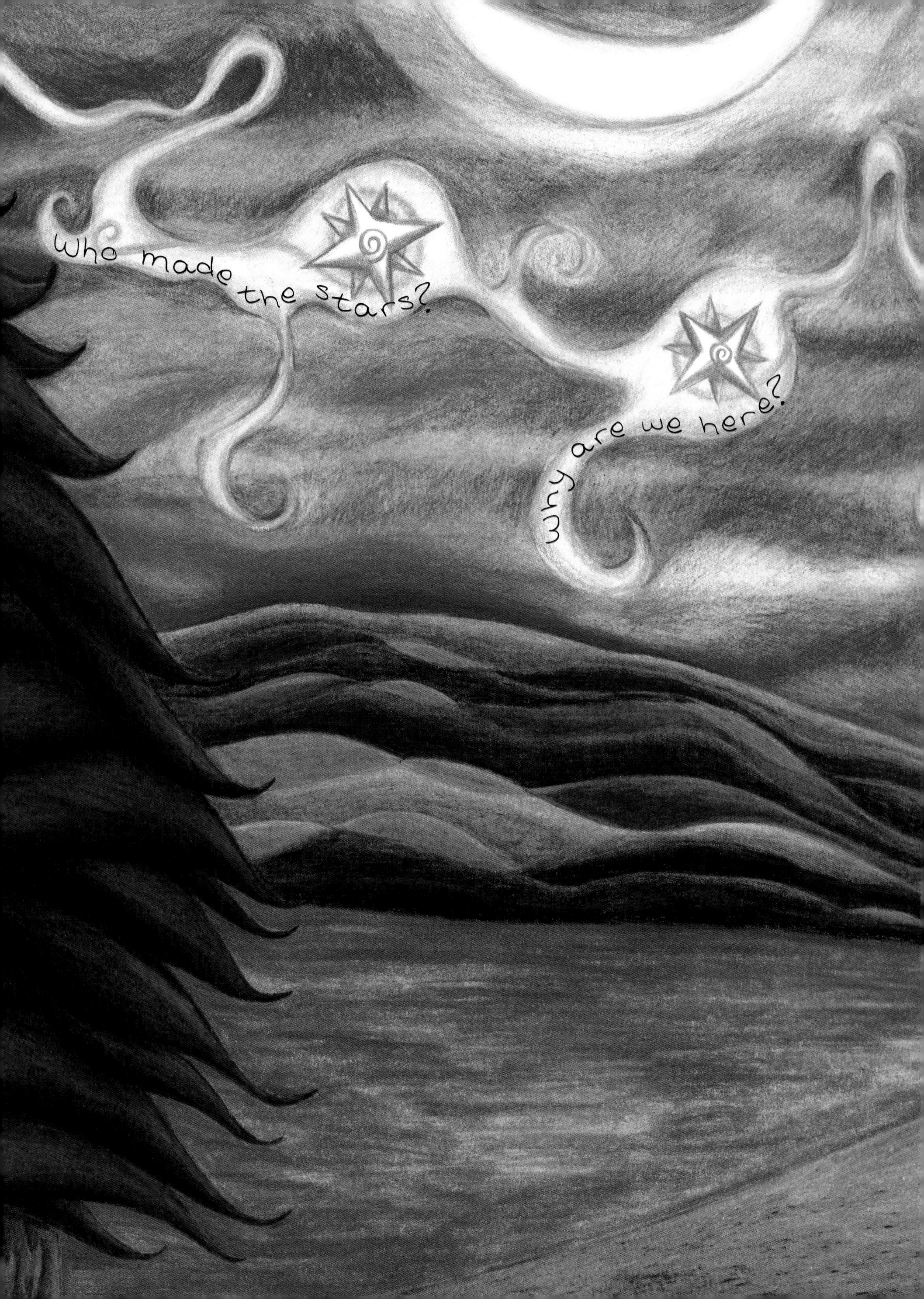
Who made the stars?
Why are we here?

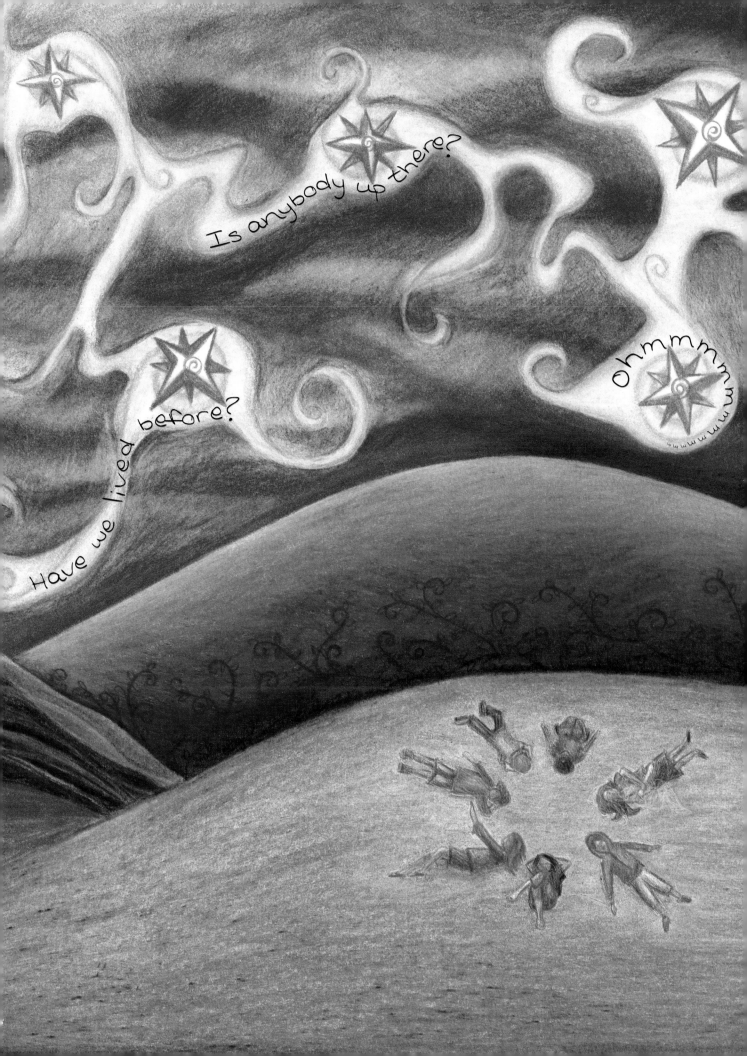

What is a Chakra, Anyway?

In the ancient Sanskrit language, the word "chakra" means "wheel." And that's what they are, really, seven spinning wheels of energy located all along the spine, or back. Let's explore each chakra's color, location, and meaning.

 Root -- Red -- Located at the base of the spine, where your bottom touches the ground when you sit. Safety, security, all the comforts of home.

 Sacral -- Orange -- Located two inches below the belly button. Creativity, new life and new ideas being born into the world, anything that feels great!

 Navel -- Yellow -- Located about two inches above the belly button. Courage and confidence -- chutzpah!

 Heart -- Green -- Located slightly to the right of, what else, your heart! Love, pure and simple.

 Throat -- Blue -- Located, surprise, surprise--right at the base of your throat! Talking, singing, laughing - any form of communication that makes *you* understood.

 Forehead -- Indigo -- Located smack dab in the middle of your forehead. Fantasy and imagination -- seeing things with your mind's eye that your other eyes can't.

 Crown -- Violet -- This is a neat one because it's the only one not located in your body at all -- it actually floats above your head! Makes sense, since this is the chakra of the spirit - that thing in all of us that is *more* than our physical body.

A Chakra Tune-Up

Feel like your chakras could use a tune-up? No problem! Find a comfy spot and sit down criss-cross-applesauce. Let your mind go all quiet and peaceful and see if you can slow down that breathing a little. Good job, now you're doing it! Now, think about the chakra you'd like to improve, and imagine that chakra's color flowing into your body, nice and gentle, like a babbling brook (not Niagra Falls, now, don't get carried away!) Continue for as long as you like. You can do this for all the chakras, or just one at a time -- your choice. You'll be surprised at the great results you get. Bet those wheels are spinning better already!